IF YOU WERE A...

Police Officer

IF YOU WERE A...
Police Officer

Virginia Schomp

BENCHMARK BOOKS

MARSHALL CAVENDISH
NEW YORK

On the ground and in the air, police officers watch over our cities and towns.

If you were a police officer, you would make sure people obey the laws. You would protect them and rescue them from danger.

Emergency! Help is needed! Who will . . .

chase the thief who robbed the restaurant?

find the lost child? the stolen car? the hidden bomb?

take a sudden, shivery leap into the icy lake to save a freezing fisherman?

Who would race to the rescue whenever help is needed? *You* would, if you were a police officer.

5

Police dogs help their partners track down and capture criminals.

The city is sleeping, but in the busy station house, the police officers are wide awake. Men and women who have worked all night are heading home, and the morning shift is checking in.

At roll call, the officers get their jobs for the day. Most will patrol the streets. Each patrol officer will protect one area of the city, called a beat. Some walk their beats with a four-legged partner. Patrol dogs are experts at sniffing out danger and helping the police collar criminals.

As a shift begins, officers find out where their help is needed.

Using his patrol car's computer, an officer checks to see if a car is stolen.

To patrol a large beat, some officers drive police cars. Riding up and down the streets, they watch for dangerous drivers and lawbreakers. When they see someone who is lost or hurt, they stop to lend a hand.

If you were a patrol officer, you might ride the city highways. On your motorcycle, you whiz right through traffic jams.

What if your beat is a busy street, beach, or boardwalk? Crowds make way when you ride your twelve hundred-pound police horse!

In different places, officers patrol in different ways—on motorcycle, on horseback, even on roller skates and snowmobiles.

While patrolling their beats, officers listen for calls on their radio or walkie-talkie. They know that in an emergency, people will phone the police station for help. The police dispatcher checks a computer map. The map shows which patrol officers are closest to the person in need.

Computers tell dispatchers where each police officer is patrolling.

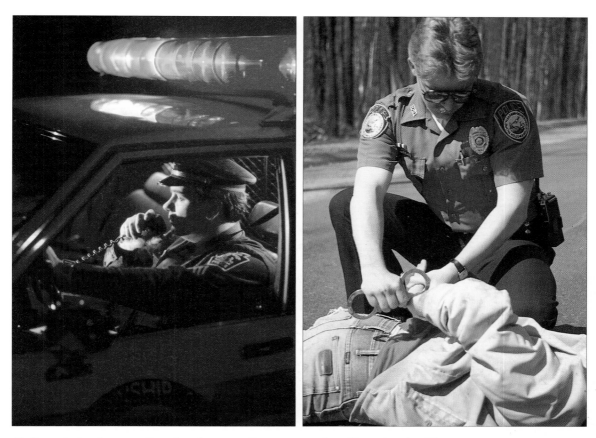

Police, 1; bad guys, 0—thanks to a fast car and well-trained officers.

The dispatcher's voice crackles through a patrol car radio. "Robbery at First Broadway Bank!" Lights flash and sirens wail as officers speed to the scene. Soon two unhappy robbers are trading stolen cash for handcuffs.

Stopping to help people in trouble is just part of a patrol officer's busy day.

What's the next emergency? If you were a patrol officer, you'd never know what to expect when the dispatcher calls.

A car has crashed! You give first aid to the driver and direct traffic around the accident. Two men are fighting! You help them use words, not fists, to settle their argument. A lost child, an injured biker—many different people may need you today. You might even help a baby who's in such a hurry to be born she won't wait till her mother gets to the hospital.

Because everyone's fingerprints are different, the prints on this glass may help detectives identify the person who broke into the house.

Police artists help catch the burglar by drawing a picture using descriptions by people who saw him.

Sometimes the police are called hours after a crime happens. No one knows who broke the law and got away. A special officer, the police detective, must try to solve the mystery.

If you were a detective, you would study clues left by the criminals—fingerprints, hairs, threads, tire marks. You would talk with many people to find out what happened. Each fact you find is another piece in the puzzle. By fitting all the facts together, you figure out who committed the crime.

With the help of a police helicopter, state troopers seize a suspected criminal.

This deputy in the Idaho countryside does many of the same jobs as a big-city patrol officer.

What other kinds of police officers do special jobs? Sheriff's deputies keep the peace in small towns that don't have a police department. While a city police officer might patrol a few busy streets, sheriff's deputies protect people and fight crime all across a county.

State troopers patrol the big state highways. They watch for speeders and help at accidents. When a lawbreaker escapes down the highway, state troopers join the chase.

A bomb suit and helmet protect an officer taking apart a deadly bomb.

Bomb squad officers are specially trained to protect people from explosions. When a dangerous-looking package is found, the bomb squad goes to work. The officers carefully examine the package. If it is a bomb, they know how to defuse it so it can't explode.

What if the bomb is hidden? Police detector dogs can find it! These super sniffers must stay quiet and calm. When a detector dog smells an explosive, it sits as still as a statue to alert its bomb squad partner.

Another special group of police officers is the SWAT team. These men and women may use powerful weapons, even tanks or explosives, to break into a building and arrest a dangerous criminal. SWAT teams also rescue hostages (HAH-stih-jihz)—innocent people taken prisoner by criminals.

This raid on a building where drugs were being made put the drug dealers out of business.

Like mountain climbers on a tall cliff, this SWAT team uses ropes to slide down a wall.

SWAT team officers are experts at using words, too. Often they can talk lawbreakers into giving themselves up. If not, the officers may have to sneak up—or down—on the criminal by climbing the sides of a tall building.

Search and rescue workers pull a drowning man from freezing waters.

Police search and rescue teams also may work in midair. Flying in helicopters, they search for people lost in mountains, deserts, and other hard-to-reach places. If you were an officer on the search and rescue team, you might hang from a rope hooked to a helicopter to rescue an injured mountain climber.

A fisherman falls into an icy lake. You leap from your police boat to save him. A missing skier? You roar to the rescue on your police snowmobile.

A police diver on a rescue mission makes a daring leap.

Most police officers help all people, young and old. But Juvenile (JOO-vuh-nyl) Officers work only with the young. These special police officers help children who have serious problems at home or school.

Sometimes an officer's most important job is being a good friend.

Classroom visits give students and officers a chance to share ideas.

Juvenile Officers may visit schools to talk about safety. Some children have fun trying out the patrol car radio and siren. The officers enjoy these visits, too. They know that boys and girls who follow safety rules make it easier for police officers to protect us all.

Do you follow safety rules? Do you like to help people? If you are strong, healthy, and honest, you could be a police officer. Men and women who want to become officers must go to a special school called the Police Academy. There they study the laws and learn how to defend themselves and help other people.

Most police officers will never use their guns, but they must know how and when to shoot.

Police Academy graduates promise to uphold the laws and treat all people honestly and fairly.

Will you earn a shiny new badge on academy graduation day? Will you join the police officers who face danger so that others can stay safe?

POLICE OFFICERS IN TIME

British police officers are nicknamed "bobbies," after Sir Robert Peel. He started the world's first modern police department, in London, England, in 1829.

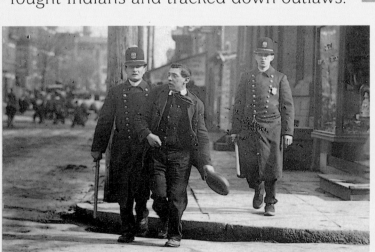

The first "state troopers" were the Texas Rangers. In the 1800s, these riflemen fought Indians and tracked down outlaws.

America's first city police department started in New York City in 1845. Other cities soon copied the idea. These officers collar a suspect in Philadelphia, Pennsylvania, in 1905.

Some early police officers patrolled the streets on bicycles.

In the early 1900s, some officers traded their pedal bikes for motorcycles—the better to catch speeders.

Once it was unusual to see a woman police officer making an arrest. Before the 1970s, most women officers handled paperwork or wrote out parking tickets.

A POLICE OFFICER'S CLOTHING AND EQUIPMENT

Police officers in different cities and towns have different-looking uniforms. Most wear a police hat and shirt, with equipment attached to a belt.

badge—for showing that someone is a police officer

gun and handcuffs—for catching dangerous criminals

walkie-talkie—for talking to police headquarters—and computer—for getting facts on people and crimes

WORDS TO KNOW

beat The area of the city or town that a police officer patrols.

defuse To take apart a bomb so it can't explode.

detector dogs Police dogs that are specially trained to search for bombs or drugs.

dispatcher The police department phone operator who answers emergency calls and sends police officers to help.

roll call The time at the police station when the officers report for work and receive their assignments for the day.

shift The part of the day that a police officer works.

This book is for Nicole, whose generous heart will bring her success on any path she chooses

Benchmark Books
Marshall Cavendish Corporation
99 White Plains Road
Tarrytown, New York 10591
Copyright © 1998 by Marshall Cavendish Corporation

Library of Congress Cataloging-in-Publication Data
Schomp, Virginia   If you were a police officer / Virginia Schomp.
p.   cm. — Includes index.
Summary: Examines the many important tasks performed by police officers as part of their jobs, including the prevention of crimes, the handling of emergencies, and the enforcement of laws.
!SBN 0-7614-0614-X (library binding)
1.Police—Juvenile literature. [1. Police. 2. Occupations.] I. Title.
HV7922.S36   1998   363.2'023'73—dc21   97-16299   CIP   AC

Photo research by Debbie Needleman

Front cover: *The Stock Market*, DiMaggio/Kalish

The photographs in this book are used by permission and through the courtesy of: *Stock Boston*: Gary Wagner, 1; Stephen Agricola, 12-13; Richard Pasley, 14. *PhotoEdit*: David Young-Wolff, 2. *The Image Works*: David Wells, 4-5; Michael Okoniewski, 6; Jim Pickerell, 7; Bob Daemmrich, 9 (left); Larry Mulvehill, 17; Dorothy Littell Greco, 19; Stephen Agricola, 20; Michael Schwarz, 24; Mark Reinstein, 27. *Gamma Liaison*: J & M Studios, 5; Daniel Simon, 9 (right); Steve Liss, 25. *David R. Frazier Photolibrary*: 8, 16, 28 (right), 30 (top). *Westlight*: Ken Rogers, 10; Dennis Degnan, 11 (left). *Leslie O'Shaughnessy*: 11 (right), 15, 18, 21, 23. *The Image Bank*: Alfred Pasieka, 14 (inset). *The Picture Cube*: L.S. Stepanowicz, 22; G. Cassidy/Camerique, 30 (bottom center). *Uniphoto Picture Agency*: Bob Daemmrich, 26. *Mary Evans Picture Library*: 28 (top left). *Culver Pictures*: 28 (bottom left), 29 (bottom). *Brown Brothers*: 29 (top and center). *William B. Folsom*: 30 (bottom left, bottom right). *Photo Researchers*: David R. Frazier, 31.

Printed in the United States of America
1   3   5   7   8   6   4   2

INDEX